DESIGN LEADERSHIP CHRONICLES

Marzia Aricò

BIS Publishers
Timorplein 46
1094 CC Amsterdam
The Netherlands
T +31 (0)20 515 02 30
bis@bispublishers.com
www.bispublishers.com
ISBN 978 90 636 9725 9
Copyright © 2024 Marzia Aricò and BIS Publishers.

Author

Marzia Aricò

Cover artwork and drawings for chapters 0, 7, 8, 9, and 10

Drawings for chapters 1, 2, and 3

Drawings for chapters 4, 5, and 6

Elena Mistrello

Gustavo Cañete

Iris Biasio

Foreword

Graphic design and layout

Editing

John Maeda

Michele Febbraio

Stu Hallybone

DESIGN LEADERSHIP CHRONICLES

A graphic novel about organisational change

Marzia Aricò

BISPUBLISHERS

A mio padre,
Che mi ha insegnato l'etica del lavoro e dimostrato che,
nella vita, tutto è possibile.

To Oliviero, Erhan, and Fulmine,
Dream big. Be humble. Now is the time to take that risk.

FOREWORD

John Maeda

In the early days at MIT's Media Lab, I was captivated by the future possibilities of design. Later, as president of Rhode Island School of Design (RISD), I delved deeply into the rich history of design. Now, in Silicon Valley, I'm fully engaged with the immediate challenges of design in the present. This journey has shown me that foresight, hindsight, and the ability to act swiftly are key qualities of a successful design leader. "Design Leadership Chronicles" reflects these themes, weaving together stories of leadership across time.

In this graphic novel, you'll encounter leaders who effectively bridge the gap between those who grasp new concepts immediately—the "get its"—and those who take more time—the "get nots." This balance is essential, especially for leaders working with 'makers' (those who create) and 'talkers' (those who articulate and advocate).

Makers thrive on creating; talkers on communicating. It's crucial for leaders, especially those leading maker teams, to understand and adapt to the predominance of talkers. Often, when makers step into leadership roles, they are seen as talkers by their peers, which can be challenging. Effective communication with product and engineering teams is vital to ensure successful outcomes for users and customers.

As you delve into this novel, each story encourages you to navigate complex environments, inspire change, and shape the future in your own role. You'll find invaluable tips on teamwork—a skill often overlooked in design education. When I transitioned from engineering to design and then to business, adapting to new team dynamics was one of my toughest challenges. I realised the importance of understanding diverse professional perspectives.

"Design Leadership Chronicles" also reminds me of a lesson from my mentor, Bill Moggridge of IDEO. He would illustrate the design process with a complex diagram of orderly steps, then contrast it with a version showing a chaotic, true-to-life flow of ideas. He simplified it by saying, "It's about starting with the people." Design happens because of the people involved. This book is your gateway to understanding and working with the many individuals you'll meet on your journey in design leadership.

CHAPTER 0
IT'S MAD OUT THERE

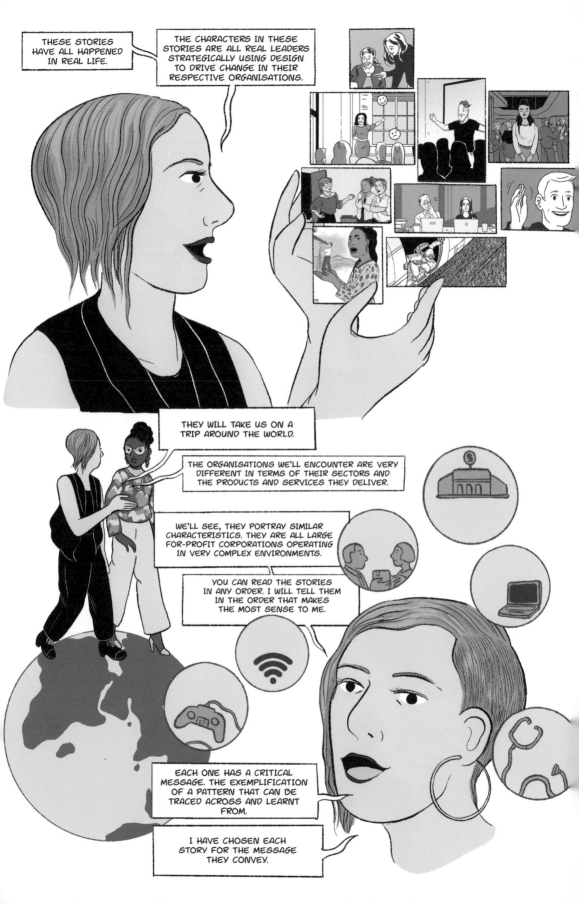

PART I

MAKING SENSE OF THE STATUS QUO

CHAPTER 1
COURTNEY MARTYN

XERO

AUSTRALIA

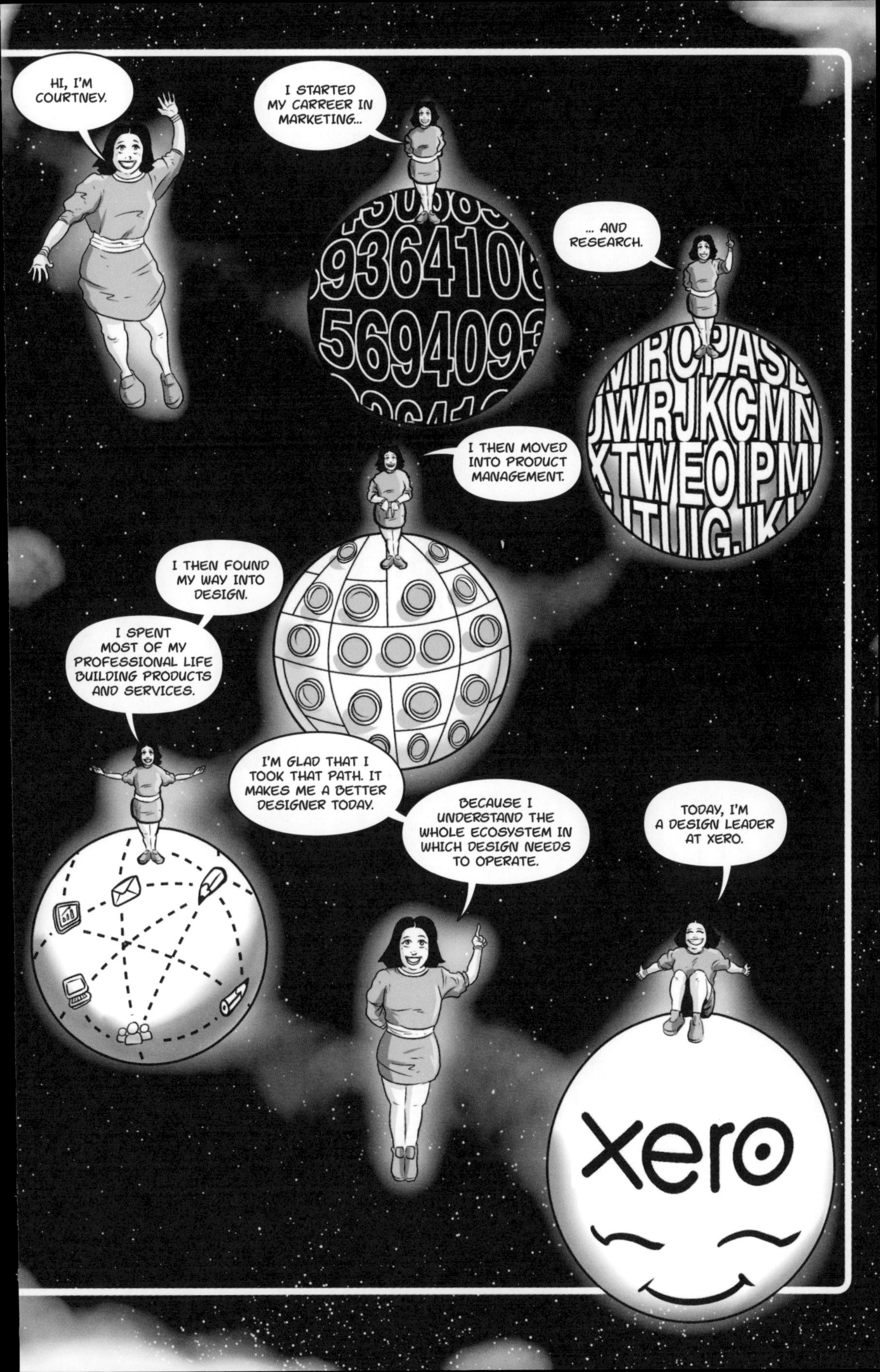
HI, I'M COURTNEY.
I STARTED MY CARREER IN MARKETING...
... AND RESEARCH.
I THEN MOVED INTO PRODUCT MANAGEMENT.
I THEN FOUND MY WAY INTO DESIGN.
I SPENT MOST OF MY PROFESSIONAL LIFE BUILDING PRODUCTS AND SERVICES.
I'M GLAD THAT I TOOK THAT PATH. IT MAKES ME A BETTER DESIGNER TODAY.
BECAUSE I UNDERSTAND THE WHOLE ECOSYSTEM IN WHICH DESIGN NEEDS TO OPERATE.
TODAY, I'M A DESIGN LEADER AT XERO.
xero

26

MAJESTY'S REVENUE AND CUSTOMS IS A NON-MINISTERIAL DEPARTMENT OF THE UK GOVERNMENT RESPONSIBLE FOR COLLECTING TAXES.

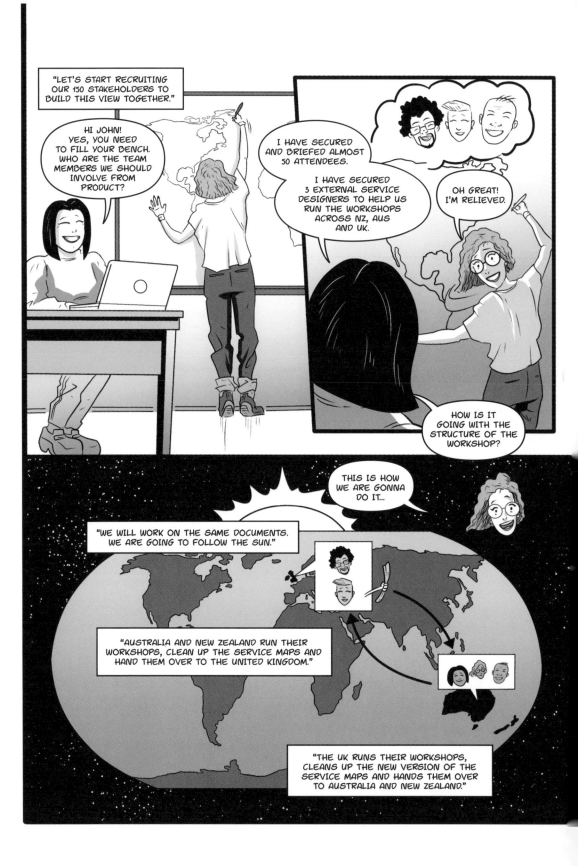

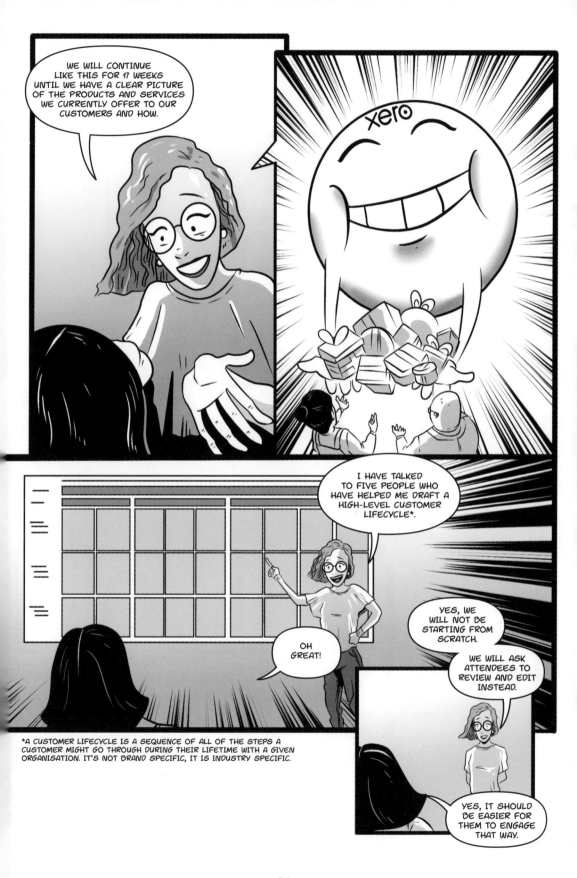

*A CUSTOMER LIFECYCLE IS A SEQUENCE OF ALL OF THE STEPS A CUSTOMER MIGHT GO THROUGH DURING THEIR LIFETIME WITH A GIVEN ORGANISATION. IT'S NOT BRAND SPECIFIC, IT IS INDUSTRY SPECIFIC.

34

35

CHAPTER 2
THOMAS FOSTER

J.P. MORGAN CHASE & CO

UK

*KEY PERFORMANCE INDICATORS

CHAPTER 3

JAAKKO TAMMELA

DASA

BRAZIL

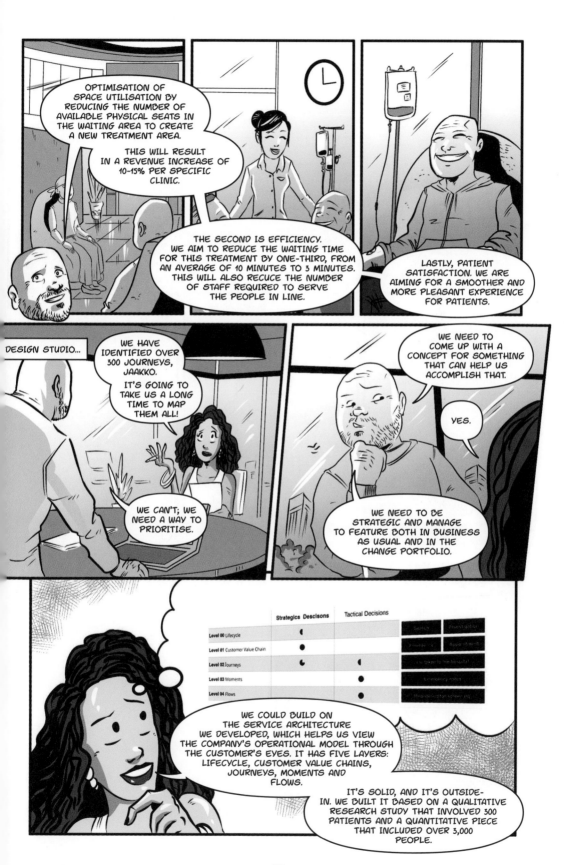

63

65

73

PART II

SEEKING CHANGE

CHAPTER 4
ALBERTA SORANZO

VODAFONE

UK

*SMALL AND MEDIUM-SIZED ENTERPRISES.

87

CHAPTER 5
NATHALIE HUNI

WELLS FARGO

USA

I'M OK TO PAY FOR YOUR TUITION BUT YOU'LL HAVE TO FIND A JOB QUICKLY AT THE END OF IT!

I KNOW...

1994. WEB AGENCY IN PARIS...

I MUST SAY I'M IMPRESSED BY YOUR PORTFOLIO NATHALIE. YOU HAVE A GOOD EYE FOR DESIGN.

WHEN CAN YOU START?

WELL, MY GRADUATION CEREMONY IS THIS THURSDAY...

... SO WHAT ABOUT MONDAY?

FIRST DAY OF WORK AT THE WEB AGENCY...

I THINK I HAVE THIS ABILITY TO LEARN VERY QUICKLY. IT'S PROBABLY DUE TO MY BACKGROUND. I MOVED A LOT AS A KID...

...WE FREQUENTLY CHANGED COUNTRIES, AND I CHANGED SCHOOLS MORE THAN I CAN COUNT. I HAD TO LEARN TO ADAPT QUICKLY.

FORTUNATELY, I'VE ALWAYS BEEN VERY CURIOUS.

NINOY AQUINO INTERNATIONAL AIRP

CANNES LIONS INTERNATIONAL FESTIVAL OF CREATIVITY, 2009...

107

CHAPTER 6
PETER BROOK

ADIDAS

GERMANY & THE NETHERLANDS

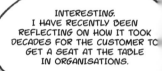

A FEW WEEKS LATER, NEW YORK, ADIDAS STORE...

YES, WE ABSOLUTELY HAVE TIME TO HELP YOU SET UP CLICK & COLLECT.

CUSTOMERS BUY ONLINE AND COLLECT THEIR PRODUCTS HERE; MAKES SENSE!

IT WORKED.

ACTUALLY, NOW THAT YOU ARE BOTH HERE, I WANTED TO SHOW YOU SOMETHING.

CLICK

TAP

TAP

TAP

TAP

WHAT'S THIS PLACE?!

WE HAVE THIS BASEMENT THAT IS PRETTY MUCH EMPTY.

THIS A PRIME SPACE IN DOWNTOWN NEW YORK!

I THOUGHT WE COULD USE IT TO SHIP FROM THE STORE.

I HEARD THAT DELIVERY TIMES IN THE NEW YORK AREA ARE LONG. WE COULD TURN THIS SPACE INTO A FULFILMENT HUB. SHIP DIRECTLY FROM HERE.

YES! THAT'S GENIUS!

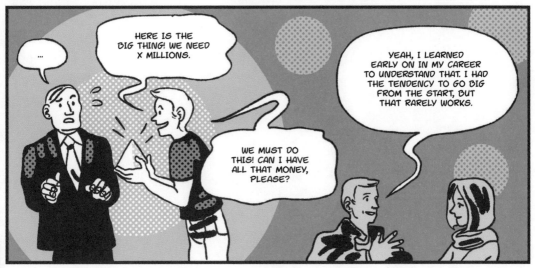

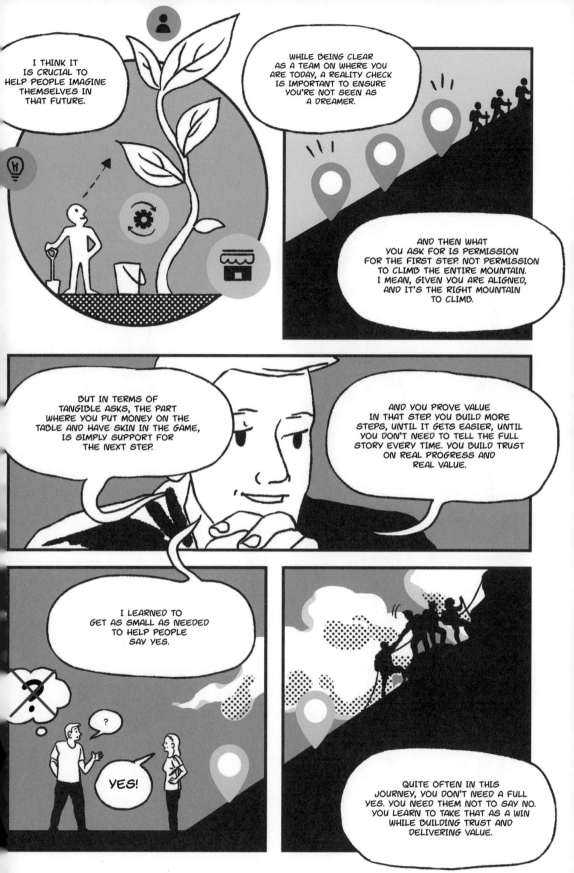

PART III

ENVISIONING ALTERNATIVE FUTURES

CHAPTER 7
HARRIET WAKELAM

INSURANCE AUSTRALIA GROUP

AUSTRALIA

YEAH, BUT THEN WHAT'S OUR ROLE AS AN ORGANISATION?

MAYBE WE SHOULD ASSESS IF WE SHOULD BE A BUILDING COMPANY.

INTERESTING, WE COULD EXPLORE THAT.

TO ME, IT'S CLEAR THAT THE BRAND PROMISE, THE PRODUCT, AND SERVICE PROMISES WE ARE BUILDING TODAY MAY NOT BE VALID IN THE FUTURE THAT IS COMING AT US.

EXACTLY!

THERE, WE CAN SEE THE SATELLITE IMAGES THAT CAN PRECISELY INDICATE THE LIKELIHOOD OF A HOUSE BEING AFFECTED BY BUSHFIRES.

COULD WE CREATE A SERVICE THAT INFORMS CUSTOMERS ABOUT THIS?

WELL, FROM A LEGAL PERSPECTIVE...

POST-WORKSHOP DEBRIEF AMONG THE DESIGN TEAM MEMBERS.

THAT WAS AMAZING!

YES, IT WAS INCREDIBLY POWERFUL.

I SAW PEOPLE BUILDING ON EACH OTHER. WE MANAGED TO INFLUENCE THE LEADERS' OUTLOOK ON THE FUTURE.

YES, I AGREE. DO YOU KNOW THE STORY OF THE WOLLEMI PINES?

MMMH, NO.

UP IN THE BLUE MOUNTAINS IN NEW SOUTH WALES, THERE IS A COLONY OF PINE TREES WHICH ARE REALLY ANCIENT.

THEY ARE THE MOST ANCIENT LIVING TREES ON THE PLANET.

CHAPTER 8

SHANI SANDY

IBM

USA

157

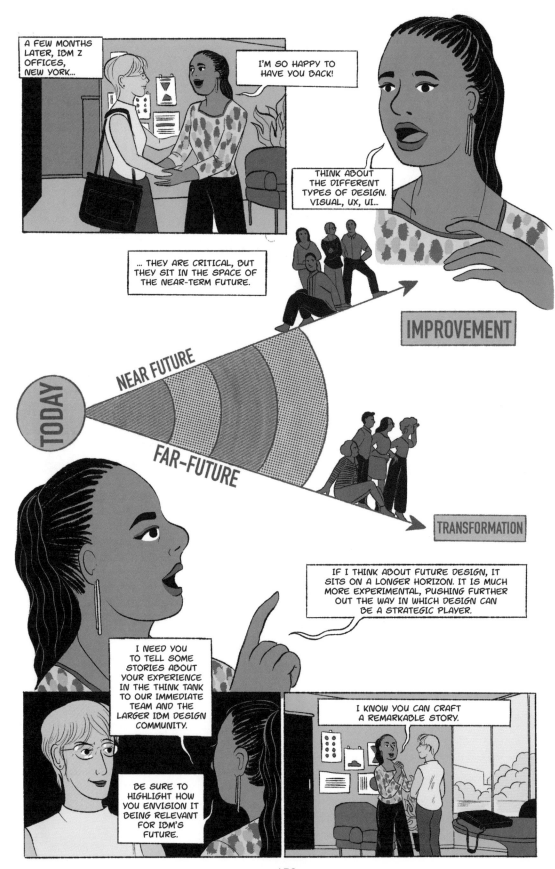

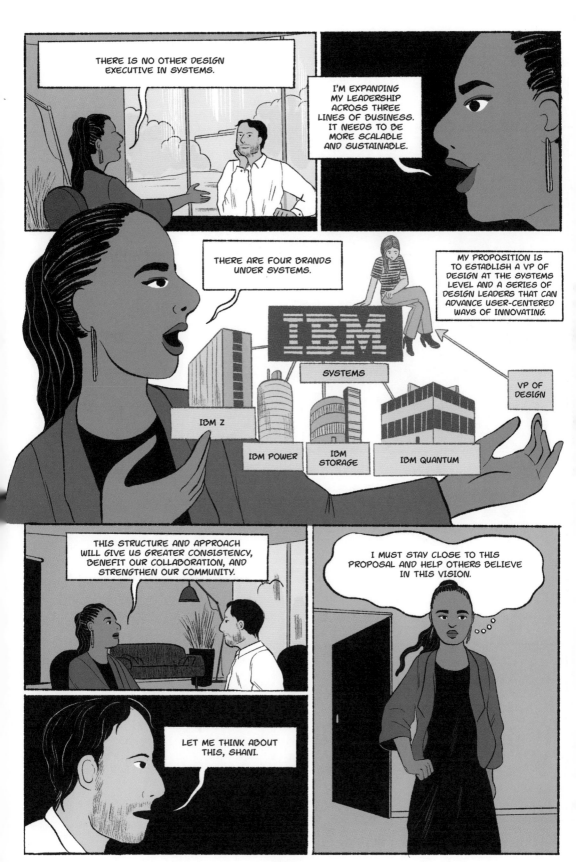

CHAPTER 9
TANARRA SCHNEIDER

ACTIVISION BLIZZARD

USA

171

172

"THEY LOVE HAVING CREATIVES AROUND BECAUSE THEY ARE SO QUIRKY AND SO DIFFERENT, THEY MAKE BEAUTIFUL THINGS, AND THEY SHAKE THINGS UP. BUT THEN THEY SAY..."

NOW GO SIT IN YOUR CORNER, AND WE'LL TELL YOU WHICH BOX WE WANT TO BE COLOURED IN WHAT COLOUR AND BY WHAT DATE.

FINALLY, I WANTED TO SLOW DOWN.

IT'S HARD TO FIND THAT IDEA INSIDE CONSULTING ORGANISATIONS WHERE EVERYTHING IS A CRISIS.

AT LEAST THAT'S HOW IT FELT.

"CLIENT FIRST, CLIENT FIRST. SO IF OUR CLIENT CHANGES SOMETHING AT THE LAST MINUTE, YOU'VE GOT TO RESPOND. AND I GOT TO THE POINT WHERE..."

ACTUALLY, I'M GONNA MAKE DINNER WITH MY KID, AND I'LL SEE YOU IN THE MORNING BECAUSE THAT'S NOT A CRISIS.

SO YOU END UP AT ODDS WITH FOLKS WHO ARE HUNGRY, THEY WANT MILLIONS OF DOLLARS IN SALES AND WOULD DO ANY TYPE OF WORK FOR THAT MONEY.

CHAPTER 10

REFLECTIONS

ACKNOWLEDGEMENTS

Since its very inception, this book has been an incredible collaborative effort. The first person I'd like to credit and thank is my good friend and colleague Angela Mancini. An early concept for this book emerged during a long night in London, where we shared ideas, experiences and intuitions while drinking red wine and eating fries. She has also been instrumental in supporting me in detailing the pilot chapter of this book, which was Tom's. Thank you for the inspiration and play.

I thank all nine professionals who have decided to share their stories openly and generously with me to be able to tell them in this book. Thank you for the trust.

I thank Kevin Corley, Ileana Stigliani, Ralitsa Diana Debrah, Alix Martínez Martínez, Emanuele Laviosa, and Manali Mohanty for actively participating in the book review committee. They have reviewed almost all chapters, always sharing useful insights to improve the work. Thank you for the constructive feedback.

I thank the Livework team for supporting the creation of the pilot chapter for this book. In particular, I thank Álvaro Curto for the art direction of the pilot chapter and Chelsea Paine for the help in finding the first graphic novel artist to work on the book.

I thank John Thackara and Kristi van Riet for hosting me in their beautiful home in Ganges (FR), and providing me with the right space and support to become serious about actually finishing this work. Thanks for your generosity, kindness and stimulating conversations.

I thank the three graphic novel artists who have believed in the project and developed all the illustrations for the book: Gustavo Cañete, Elena Mistrello, and Iris Biasio. Thank you for the patience and dedication to produce something we can all be proud of.

I thank Stu Hallybone, who has reviewed and helped edit the entire copy of the book. Thank you for being of great practical and emotional support at key moments of this journey.

I thank Michele Febbraio for the graphic design, composition and cover design. Thank you for the attention to detail.

I thank my Mum, Dad and Sister, who have always believed I could do anything in life, to the point that I started to believe that myself very early on. I never stopped believing in that.

I thank my husband Jonas, who has been encouraging me, supporting me and providing feedback throughout the creation of this book. Thank you for being there in all the good ways you know.

Finally, Oliviero, Erhan, and Fulmine, thank you for making me want to be a better person every single day. You are infinite.

P.S.
Fulmine, my love, we'll soon decide what your real name is. It will be a great one, I promise.

BIOGRAPHIES

Gustavo Cañete is a comic artist based in Argentina. He has been passionate about drawing since childhood, creating his own comics and dreaming of a career in the industry. After studying at "La Ola" comic school, he began working on numerous global projects, collaborating with talented artists and storytellers. Gustavo has partnered with Mark Millar at Far Future Enterprises on an upcoming comic about travellers, a classic RPG board game. In Argentina, he works on "Lucha Fuerte", a comic inspired by an '80s wrestling show, and "Soul of Warriors". He has also contributed to various international webcomics.

Iris Biasio is a comic artist and illustrator who founded the NeroVite project in 2016, using drawing and storytelling to craft numerous short comic narratives. In July 2022, Rizzoli Lizard published her debut book, "Mia sorella è pazza," which earned her the Boscarato Prize at the Treviso Comic Book Festival. In 2023, she received accolades including a special mention for Best Debut at the Micheluzzi Awards, won the Bartoli Prize for Best Promise in Italian Comics at Rome's ARF! Festival, and secured the Gran Guinigi for Best Debutant at Lucca Comics & Games. Biasio also collaborates with various publishers and teaches comic and illustration workshops regularly.

Elena Mistrello, an illustrator and comic artist, collaborates with various Italian and international magazines and publishers. In 2022, she published "Sindrome Italia" with Tiziana Vaccaro, winning "Best Screenplay" at TCBF and "Best Debut Work" at Napoli Comicon, along with the "Bookciak, Azione!" award at the Venice Film Festival. In 2023, she published "Tracciato Palestina," winning the BICA award for "Best Single Work" at Belgioso Comics and Games. Additionally, in 2023, she collaborated with Avsi on "Ripartire dai resti," a comic reportage about Ukrainian refugee women in Poland.